Foraging:

Top 20 Seasonal Wild Foods to Forage

Table of content

Introduction

Nature gifts free food in the wilderness that is often used for environmental and medicinal benefits. Foraging for food is really beneficial for everyone because you can get healthy vegetables and herbs. Herbal medicine can be obtained from oceans, farmlands, wilderness, and park. In the wilderness foraging, you can get leafy greens, sea vegetable, berries, flowers, mushrooms, nuts and various other herbs and vegetables. You can get food with all six tastes, such as bitter, sweet, pungent (spicy), salty, astringent (drying) and sour. Maximum people are dependent on agriculture for the majority of their food, but it is fun to get self-sufficiency in food. Foraging has lots of physical and spiritual health benefits.

Foraging is handy for those who loves walking and camping. They can find herbs and plants to get energy. These herbs and plants can be used to make fritters, salads, sauces, sandwiches, pesto, teas and herbal medicines. It is extremely important to identify the plant before using it. There are many plants that look similar to each other; therefore, you should identify edible and poisonous plants. It is essential to learn that which part of your selected plant is edible. Before foraging, you have to learn its general and safety rules. It is essential to honor all plants and avoid excessive picking. Keep it in mind that animals survive on these plants and there should be something behind to reproduce this plant and keep the ecosystem alive.

Before harvesting any plant, learn its particular procedure because leaves, roots, and flower play an important role in the lifecycle of plants. For instance, flower, fruit, and leaves are good to gather during summer and the roots are good during fall. Be aware of your safety because there are a few poisonous plants that can kill you or some may trigger dermatitis and allergic reactions. Make sure to identify plants before gathering them. You should ensure that you are not harvesting from an area with water and air pollution. It is essential to collect details about any kind of pesticides sprayed on the plant. You shouldn't forage for commercial reasons. Try to get legal permission to start foraging in any particular area.

This book is designed for your guidance so that you can learn foraging and its rules. You can read information about seasonal foraging.

Chapter 1 – Getting Started with Edible Wild Plants

The foraging for wild food is quickly gaining popularity because it is really exciting to discover new foods and save your money. You can get free and delicious leaves, nuts, seeds, fruits and roots that are available in your garden and backyard, so go and get them. But wait, there are some safety rules and etiquettes for foraging that should be considered before starting anything:

Initially, Stay Closed to Your Home

If you are going out to get wild plants that are growing closer in your areas, you can go to search, but make sure to stay close to your home. Use your observation skills to determine either the area is sprayed with herbicides or heavy fertilizers. If the plants are curled down and discolored in an unnatural manner, it can be the sign of chemical use. It will be good to avoid this area. In the same way, if you want to forage in your own garden, you should avoid those areas where you may use heavy pesticides.

Don't Travel on Populated Road

If you want to forage on a populated road, it is a bad idea because the plants in a populated area may soak up exhaust fumes and pollutants from vehicles. These are not good for your health and will not taste good. You should look for plants at least 100 feet away from the road.

Information About Plants and Herbs

Before starting your foraging journey, it will be good to collect sufficient information about edible wild plants in your area and learn to identify them. Keep it in mind that there are some toxic herbs and plants growing in wild areas. You have to be careful about these plants and herbs.

Avoid Over Harvesting

You can't harvest plants until you now the noxious status of the weeds and plants. It will be good to take 1/3rd of a plant and your selected plant should be plentiful in numbers in the designated area. If you see only a few plants, you should avoid their harvesting.

Start Small

If you are eating a particular food item for the first time, you should start with small quantity. Eat the food in small amounts to let your body adjust to the new food. You may have allergies with a specific food and this step will help you to avoid any major problem.

Start Working in Group

As a beginning forager, you should work in groups and get sufficient experience. You should work under the guidance of an expert mentor who can guide you about the nature of plants and the ways to identify them.

Start With Local Fields

You can get the advantage of a local field guide for foraging because this guide will help you to recognize edible plants. Initially, you can select three plants that grow well in your area and study about their leaves, flowers, stems, shapes and habits. You can start with berries and mushrooms.

Symptoms of Harmful Plants

There are some poisonous plants in your areas, such as poison sumac, ivy, and nettles that are growing in your area. These can be identified with a horrible sting. These may leave you with unexpected rash and can damper your foraging adventures. You should write the lookalike and properties of poisonous plants in your diary. It will be a good idea to write descriptions of plants and click images so that you can compare them for the future.

Don't Focus on Myths

Keep it in mind that your safety is really important; therefore, you can't rely on myths. You can't taste a plant to identify it because it can be dangerous. There are some myths about the foraging of food, so be careful about them. Some common myths are:

- Edible plants are easy to identify for their good taste, while the poisonous plants only taste bad.

- If animals are eating these plants, it means these are safe.

- It is okay to perform an edibility test on the plants to check it.

Unfortunately, these all myths are really dangerous because some poisonous plants really taste good than edible plants. It doesn't mean to cook a poisonous plant for its good taste. The kohlrabi or Brussels sprouts have weird taste, but these are safe to eat. Some experienced foragers can make mistakes in the identification of plants. The wild carrot, goldenrod and hemlock and ragweed are some examples of poisonous plants. The animals can make the mistake to eat poisonous plants as well; hence, you can't trust animals while foraging for food.

You should leave enough plants so that the population of this plant can recover. There is no need to over-harvest after seeing a plentiful plant because this action can stop their growth.

Chapter 2 – Foraging Plants in Summer

Foraging is summer will be an interesting way to get tasty lemons, berries, mushrooms and other food items. Foraging is a great way to establish a deep relation with nature. In summer, you can forage different kinds of berries, fruits, leaves, and flowers. There are a few wild foods that you can forage in summer:

Plant 01: Lemon Balm (Melissa Officinalis)

This plant is easy to identify for its oval hairy leaves and toothed edges. These leaves are opposite on one square and the breached stems can grow 1m in the late summer. You can crush these leaves to feel the smell of lemon. This plant has small and two-lipped flowers in white, yellow or pink colors. these flowers are available in clusters and the bees love these flowers.

You can pick the young leaves because the older leaves are harsh and tough. This can be used raw as a salad or to make pesto. You can chop them to add in ricotta, cream cheese and mayonnaise. You can infuse them in vinegar or custard or enjoy a cup of tea. These leaves can be bruised to flavor punches and wine cups. You can use old leaves or stems on the barbecue. It is a garden escapee because these may be wasted on the ground of garden too.

Plant 02: Borage (Borago Officinalis)

Spiny and hairy leaves in oval shape are 25cm long and these leaves taste like a cucumber. You can notice five-petaled and star-shaped blue flowers. You can pick flowers by gripping their black stamen and pull the flower off its green calyx. The flowers are found in nodding clusters on the plant that is almost 30cm to 1m tall. You will notice it on the ground next to allotments and garden.

You can use small leaves and beautiful flowers in salads. Large leaves can be used to flavor butter and olive oil. this plant can be used as side vegetables or with pasta and ricotta. You can serve with mayonnaise for chicken and fish. Sprig of borage is used to flavor your beers and wine. It is traditionally known as "Cool Tankard" and the flowers are often used to garnish desserts and Pimm's.

Plant 03: Berries

You can forage for a few varieties of wild berries that can be cooked in tarts and pies or can be consumed as a whole fruit. The berries have vitamins and minerals along with quick energy sugar. You can find berries everywhere in North America, United States, and Canada. These are typically found on the ground creepers and low bushes. There are different types of edible berries, such as strawberries, blackberries, wineberries, cherries, raspberries, etc. that can be foraged in your garden or backyard easily. In this book, you will find methods to forage berries along with common mistakes to avoid.

Berries are great wild foods that can be consumed by fruits or some species needed to be cooked in tarts and other desserts. Berries look really attractive and tasty, but you should be careful before selecting berries because there are lots of poisonous berries there too. There are some tips that can help you in the foraging of berries:

- You can't eat berries unless you are completely sure that it is edible for you.

- A bird eating berries can't be a guarantee that it is safe for you to eat. The birds can eat lots of berries that are toxic to you.

- You should avoid foraging for berries in the areas with heavy pesticides or near polluted rivers, industrial areas, and roads.

- Children often feel tempted to eat wild berries, but it is important to teach them how to identify berries found in your area or backyard.

- The berries may ripen during summer and fall and these are easy to identify. Before foraging for any types of berries, make sure to check the legal status of your area about berries.

- It will be good to get foraging classes offered by the horticulture group or an institution to identify wild and edible berries and other plants.

Foraging for berries is a great outdoor activity that you can enjoy with your family to appreciate nature. You should take time and study about berries to make this activity rewarding and secure.

Plant 04: Origanum vulgare (Oregano)

This native plant grows in hedges, dry grassland, and woodland edges. You can recognize this plant with its oval and hairy leaves. These leaves are stalked and toothed. Before growing flowers, it looks like one low bush or almost 20 to 40 cm. The flower spikes may grow to almost 75cm. the flowers are purple-pinky in clusters. It is used dried or fresh in tomato and pizza sauces. It can be infused in wine vinegar. You can pick its dry stalks, bunch, and flower from the airy place. Crush the dry leaves and buds of flowers to use in winter.

All petals of roses are edible, but you should be careful and avoid sprayed varieties. The wild rose is found in wild places and hedges. The flowers grow up to 3m and have curved thorns. The flowers are 4 to 5 cm across with five petals and you can get flowers from June – July. Pick these flower as they started to drop.

The field roses are similar and smaller to almost 1, with white petals. Raw petals can be used in salads and infuse in vinegar to make crystallize or jam. You can dry flowers to use in Asian and Middle Eastern dishes.

Chapter 3 – Foraging Plants for Winter

Foraging in winter sounds like a hard work because of the wet and cold season. In winter, you should wear waterproof gloves and boots. If you want to forage plants in winter, there are a few options for you:

Plant 06: Oyster Mushrooms

This mushroom is easy to found at any time of a year. As the name suggests, oyster mushrooms look similar to a bunch of oysters. They grow in layers on deciduous wood. These mushrooms are white and hairless. Oyster mushrooms can be found in November or even December. This is just like a treasure in the woods and these are easy to identify. They have a beautiful shape and grow on the beach. They are grey in color and have no gills. There is another genus of oyster mushrooms, but these will taste different. You can use these mushrooms in soups, stews and stir-frying.

Plant 07: Chanterelles

This golden and yellowish mushroom is easy to spot while walking in the woods. The morels are better known for their unique properties, peachy and peppery flavor.

Growth Place

They grow on the east and west coastlines. The chanterelles on The East coast can become smaller in size than the mushroom on the west coast. The size of the chanterelles on the east coast can be almost equal to a fist and the weight of the west coast mushroom is two pounds.

Time to Forage

You can forage in summer and fall in the East Coast and the September to February are good to grow on the West Coast. You should look for this type around conifers on West Coast and on East Coast, they are found around hardwoods, such as oak species.

The chanterelles grow in clusters among conifers, hardwood, bushes, and shrubs. You can find them among mosses and grasses.

Cookery Uses

The fleshy mushrooms are good for cooking because you can slice them in generous-sized slices to get maximum flavor. These are good to sauté in cream, butter, chicken broth and oil. They are good for stews and soups along with chicken and veal.

Stinging nettles can be noticed in winter and these are heart-shaped leaves have stinging hair on them. They make a super nutritious and delicious diet. They can be found in woodlands, grazing land and on hedge banks. Their rich green color indicates that they are extremely high in chlorophyll and iron. They are high in minerals, Sulphur, silicon, zinc, magnesium, phosphorus and cobalt. Make sure to pick young plants because old plants can be fibrous and bitter in taste. You can cut the top 4 to 6 inches of this plant so that it can regrow easily.

Plant 09: Navelwort

The name navelwort derives from its shape that is similar to the belly button. It can easily survive during the winter season. It tastes great in salads and sandwiches. But make sure you pick more of younger leaves as mature leaves tend to have a more bitter taste. It is frequently used for medicinal purposes and you can get the advantage of this plant as well.

This plant is dense and has lots of branches and shrub. This is an evergreen plant, but its lives are minute and fall off at the earliest time. Some older plants may form long and thread-like sharp spines that will be straight and furrowed. Some gorse is mostly in flower. It is found in open lush areas, sunny sights and sandy soil. Gorse has yellow colored eye catching flower which can be eaten raw or used in salads and can also be used to make fruit tea. The golden flowers of this plant are really powerful to use in perfumes. These flowers often open in early spring almost in August or later. This plant is available for a whole year. You can take its flowers or spikes, but make sure to wear gloves before foraging them.

Chapter 4 – Foraging Guide for Autumn

After a warm and hot summer, you can enjoy the tastes and advantages of plants and herbs in autumn. Plants will garner blimey that will be stored in fruits in the winter season. You can get the advantage of various plants and herbs. There are a few plants and foods that you can forage in autumn:

Plant 11: Lion's Mane Mushrooms

These are edible mushrooms for foragers and these are famous for their bearded tooth and pom pom structure. These are easily found in the hardwood trees in the late fall and summer. Its unique shape is quite similar to the mane of a lion or pom pom. The taste of this mushroom is quite similar to seafood.

Tips to Recognize Them

You can find them near beech trees and these often grow its spines from one group instead of branches. It can grow in high trees at a 40 feets high trunk.

Plant 12: Maitake Mushrooms

It is famously known as the hen of the forest and these can be found at the bottom of hardwood, such as oaks. It is famous in the Northeast, but can be found in the west as Idaho. The large mushrooms can be difficult to eat. It is important to harvest them as they are young. It can be dried to make powders to use in sauces, soups and bread.

These are easy to recognize for their small and overlapping shaped caps.

Plant 13: Rose Hips (Rosa Species)

In the summer, you will look at flowers, but in the autumn season, you can get a bonus in the shape of hips. Rose hips are filled with vitamin C, such as the hips of field rose and dog rose. Hips of these rose have pointed oval shape with 2-centimeter length. These may vary in color, such as green to bright red. If you want to get rose hips, make sure to wear gloves to protect your hands from thrones. These may contain irritating hair that should be removed before processing them. The hips can be strained through one jelly bag to make jelly or syrup. You can blend this powder in ginger, lemon, cardamom, and almonds.

These trees are deciduous and 10 meters tall. The true crab has throne with cupped flowers and toothed leaves. Fruits are almost 2 centimeters in diameter and round in shape. You can notice a star shape after cutting them horizontally. This fruit has a tart and available in a variety of colors. They start ripening from October. These are high in pectin; therefore, you can use them to make jellies and jams. You can mix them with low pectin fruit, such as rose hips, blackberries and rowan berries. Apple jelly can be prepared with herbs, such as savory, basil, and mint.

Plant 15: Blackberry

Blackberry is quite unique for its archines canes and open spaces in the tangled thickets. The first fruit can be obtained at the end of each cane and this fruit will be pulpy and sweet. You can use them in the preparation of bramble jelly, jam, and pies. These are also used in the preparation of whiskey and wine. You can try these berries with cheese and syrupy vinegar in ice cream and dressings.

Chapter 5 – Foraging Guide for Spring

You can get the actual pleasure of foraging in spring because there will be numerous choices for you. In the spring, your foraging will get new dimensions:

Plant 16: Primrose

These striking flowers are really special and available in the United Kingdom. These can self-seed in garden easily and their flowers are almost 2 to 3 crossways. Flowers have five petals and oval leaves can be noticed on the stalk. Use leave and flowers to garnish your salads or fry leaves in olive oil to make them crispy.

Plant 17: Sambucus nigra (Elder)

In early summer, you can notice white umbels and these look very beautiful. You can find them in woods and waste places of the cities. Its shrub has long stemmed with cracked bark and dark grey pores. These leaves contain 3 to 9 leaflets in opposite direction along the stem. You can use berries of flowers because rest of the plant is poisonous. These beautiful scented flowers can be used to make wine, vinegar, cordial, and fritters. These flowers turn magical in strawberry jam.

These are easily available in the grassy fields and waste places. Cut their parts and you will notice a milky sap; therefore, it is essential to wear gloves and avoid stains on hands. You can notice that the leaves are growing from its base and the flowers are on the hollow stalks. The leaves of this plant can be bitter like chicory. You can use spring leaves to avoid a bitter taste. These leaves can be used as spinach or salad taste. Buds of flowers are good to make fritters, such as coat them in batter and fry.

This is an all-pervasive weed and lots of people may already know it. It is one of the weeds that frequently grow in your garden or backyard. Unfortunately, the dandelion grown in your backyard and lawn may not fit for the consumption because of the chemicals that you are using for the protection of your garden. The flowers, leaves, and roots are edible because you can cook it just like spinach and add to sandwiches and salads. It has lots of vitamins C, potassium, and calcium. It can be one of good mineral sources and antioxidant. It helps you to clean your kidneys, liver, and the urinary bladder.

It is a ground hugging herb and it is easy to miss because of its growing patterns. You can notice it growing almost everywhere, in exposed areas, where nothing grows. The tiny leaves, pink, plump stems and yellow flowers are edible. They have a slightly sour taste and you can enjoy them raw or cooked. They are a good source of Vitamin A, C, and E along with the number of other minerals. If you want plenty of Omega-3 fatty acids, these are good sources for you.

Plant 20: Garlic mustard (Alliaria Petiolata)

Garlic mustard is also known as Jack-by-the-Hedge, as they are found in the hedgerows, sideways or on the corners of a timberland. Garlic mustard also has heart shaped leaves. Their leaves are shiny and hairless. They also have a strong smell of garlic but not as strong as Ramsons. The aftertaste of a garlic mustard can be bitter if only its leaf is eaten. It is best when you mix it as an ingredient with salad.

You can also use garlic mustard for stuffing foods such as a small trout or any other fish. The garlic mustard plant is fully developed in later spring and can be easily identified. The leaves of garlic are perfect for cooking like spinach or making pesto with it. You can recognize it by its smell, broad leaves and tender buds of flowers on the long stalks. The leaves may have a slightly bitter taste, but you can consume them easily.

Chapter 6 – Washing and Storing Tips for Foraged Food

If you want to store your mushrooms for one week or more, you should store fresh mushrooms and place in a brown paper bag. You should store them unwashed, and fold the top of the bag over. Now keep the bag in the main compartment of your refrigerator. The brown paper bag can absorb surplus dampness from the mushrooms. It will prevent any mold or soggy texture of the mushrooms.

Tips to Store Mushrooms

- It is not good to store mushrooms in the crisper drawer because it is a moist environment.

- The mushrooms should not be placed near foods with strong flavors and odors. These can absorb them just like a dab.

- Some mushrooms can stay in the fridge in a better way than others. If you want to store mushrooms for one week or more, it will be good to freeze or dry them.

Tips to Store Berries

After foraging for berries, there are some tips that can help you to keep your berries fresh:

- After bringing berries home, you can use pH vinegar to keep them fresh by killing spores on the fruit.

- Use vinegar-water bath to remove any dirt, kill bacteria and spore and remove grime from the berries.

- Use a colander to drain the berries and rinse the fruit well. You can use a salad spinner to dry the fruit with thick skin. You can use a towel to dry raspberries and blackberries.

- Store properly washed and dry fruits in a sealed pot lined with a dry paper towel. You should use an air-tight pot and leave the lid slightly open to avoid build-up of natural moisture.

Tips to Keep Your Berries and Other Fruits Fresh

A quick bath with hot water can be a good choice, such as keep strawberries, blackberries and raspberries for 30 seconds in 125-degree water. The blueberries can be kept for 30 seconds at 140 degrees' water. It will kill bacteria and clean your berries.

You can use a commercial cleaner, such as EatCleaner or others can be a good choice to clean and fresh berries and increase their life by keeping in the refrigerator.

Washing as well as Storing Tips for Summer Berries

There are some tips that can help you to store the summer berries for a longer period of time:

- It is important to rinse the berries before using them because the water can increase the chances of mold.

- You can't soak berries and keep them in a colander while rinsing with water. The soaking can increase the chances of mold.

- The warm berries will not feel good so you can keep them in the refrigerator for a quick chill. The sun-ripened berries have pleasant soft scruffiness. These can be difficult to wash so it will be good to keep in the refrigerator for an hour to make them hard.

- After washing your berries, you can keep them in a colander and then in the refrigerator. This can encourage air circulation and help it dry out easily.

- Some people think that the berries may become worse after keeping in the crisper because of the high humidity in the air.

With the help of given tips and tricks, you can forage for mushrooms and berries. These are good for you to store for a longer period of time and enjoy in soups, stews, and desserts. These will be used similarly in cooking as you use other mushrooms available in the market. These are good to save money and include essential nutrition in your staple diet.

Conclusion

Foraging is referred as an act of finding and harvesting wild food, but you can do it in your backyard. The foraging depends on location and one can easily forage wild rice, mangoes, buts, ramps, plums, nettles, persimmons, dandelion greens, dill, and berries. There are plenty of edible herbs and vegetables around you that can be enjoyed. Foraging for edible herbs and plants is an old technique and this can be an interesting activity to get free food full of nutritious. It is a fact that wild plants are far better than commercially cultivated plants because you can get a variety of nutritious in foraged food that is missing in your staple diet.

The surprising flavor and unusual textures, unique colors and nutritional value can give a new life to your cooking. Keep it in mind that different landscapes produce different plants. If you are in a mowed lawn, you can find chickweed, sheep sorrel, dandelion and pineapple weed. If there is a meadow behind your house, you can find milkweed, oxeye daisies and wild garlic in the high grasses. In wooded areas, you can garlic mustard, different kinds of berries, wintergreen, sassafras, mayapple and California bay. The choices are unlimited because you can grow food in different settings.

If you are curious to learn more about foraging, this book can be a good place to start. In this book, will receive a comprehensive guide to the foraging process, its safety, and a procedure to grow berries and edible mushrooms. Read this book because it has lots of important things important for you to learn.

FREE Bonus Reminder

If you have not grabbed it yet, please go ahead and download your special bonus report *"DIY Projects. 13 Useful & Easy To Make DIY Projects To Save Money & Improve Your Home!"*

Simply Click the Button Below

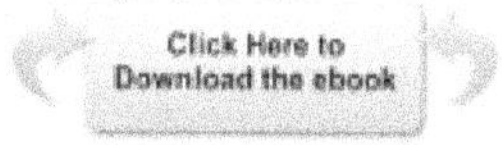

OR Go to This Page

http://healthylivingpeople.com/free/

BONUS #2: More Free & Discounted Books

Do you want to receive more Free & Discounted Books?

We have a mailing list where we send out our new Books when they go free or with a discount on Kindle. Click on the link below to sign up for Free & Discount Book Promotions.

=> Sign Up for Free & Discount Book Promotions <=

OR Go to this URL

www.ingramcontent.com/pod-product-compliance
Lightning Source LLC
Chambersburg PA
CBHW050803240726
48654CB00008B/617